MAC & MADI'S SU

A Very Different Twins Birthday

By Linda Herron

Illustrated By Marie Delon

MAC & MADI'S SURPRISE: A VERY DIFFERENT TWINS BIRTHDAY!

First edition May 2019 Book design by Project 100

ISBN: 9781733321709

www.lherron.com

Publisher's Cataloging-In-Publication Data
(Prepared by The Donohue Group, Inc.)

Names: Herron, Linda, author. | Delon, Marie, illustrator.
Title: Mac & Madi's surprise : a very different twins birthday! / by Linda Herron ; illustrated by Marie Delon.
Other Titles: Mac and Madi's surprise
Description: First edition. | [San Jose, California] : [Big Little Press], 2019. | Series: [Twins, Mac & Madi] ; [book 1] | Interest age level: 003-008. | Summary: Mac and Madi are identical twins who manage at a young age to realize and accept their differences. They decide together to share their birthday jubilation with a surprise for family and friends.
Identifiers: ISBN 9781733321716 (hardcover) | ISBN 9781733321709 (paperback) | ISBN 9780578523132 (ebook)
Subjects: LCSH: Twins--Juvenile fiction. | Birthdays--Juvenile fiction. | Individual differences--Juvenile fiction. | CYAC: Twins--Fiction. | Birthdays--Fiction. | Individual differences--Fiction.
Classification: LCC PZ7.1 .H49465 Ma 2019 (print) | LCC PZ7.1 .H49465 (ebook) | DDC [E]--dc23

For all Twins,
"May you hug, smile and laugh throughout
your life with your best friend."
– Linda Herron

Mac and Madi look the same.

Same hair.
Same smile.
Same size.

Mac

Madi

And when they laughed, same scrunched
up crinkly nose and eyes.

The twins were so famous for being identical
that their friends even got them confused.

But the twins were not only famous for being the same.

Their birthday parties were famous too!

Every year they held a big bash:

Same cake. Same colors.
Same food. Same clothes.

But Mac and Madi were tired of the same old.
This year was going to be different.

The twins had a plan,
and their birthday traditions were about to change.

At the bakery, Mac chose German Chocolate and
Madi chose Vanilla Funfetti.

At the party store, Madi chose purple
and Mac chose yellow.

At the grocery store, Mac chose pizza
and Madi chose tacos.

At the mall, Mac chose pants and Madi chose shorts.

On their birthday, Mac and Madi woke early and quietly said, "Today is our day."

But Madi thought,
"I wonder if Mom and Dad are going to be upset."

Mac puzzled, "I wonder if our friends will fret."

But when it was time to celebrate...

Their friends were shocked.

Mom and Dad's eyes locked.

Nothing was the same!

Different cake. Different colors.
Different food. Different clothes.
Silence ensued...

And then, everyone hugged.

Happy Birthday Madi!

Happy Birthday Mac!

Mac and Madi were still the same.

Same hair.
  Same smile.
    Same size.

And when they laughed, same scrunched up crinkly nose and eyes. But now, as they say,

"We love being different even though
we are similar in many ways!"

Author: Linda Herron

Born and raised in Rhode Island, Linda Herron knows firsthand what it is like to grow up as an identical twin. In fact, the most wonderful part of her childhood was spending time with her best friend and twin sister.

Because Linda recognizes the unique bond—and the unique challenges—that being a twin entails, she was inspired to create a series of children's stories about being an identical twin. Her latest book is Mac & Madi's Surprise: A Very Different Twins Birthday!

When she isn't writing children's books, Linda spends some of her time writing business articles and blogs. As the CEO of SimpliProfit, she provides strategic advising that transforms businesses by boosting profitability. Her financial expertise has been featured on media outlets including American Express, LendingTree, and Daily Business News, and she holds a bachelor's degree in accounting from Bryant University.

Today, Linda lives in California and enjoys the sunny, seventy-five-degree weather every day. Though her twin still lives in Rhode Island, they visit each other to spend time together.

If you'd like to learn more, purchase books, or join her mailing list, you can connect with Linda via her website or her Instagram, Facebook, and Twitter accounts.

PARENT GUIDE: by Barbara Klein, Ph.D.
Developing Unique Interests in Your Twin Children

Raising twins is a major ongoing challenge for parents, close relatives, and teachers. In addition to the life-sustaining importance of physical care, the emotional attention and psychological mindfulness required for raising twins can be complicated and stressful. In my experience working with parents of twins, feeling exhausted or overwhelmed is a very normal reaction.

For these reasons, asking parents to react to each child as a unique individual may sound like too much work, especially at first, but making a special connection with each of your children will pay off in the long run. Fighting will be reduced—and you will be better able to understand what is going on when it does happen. The competition will be less intense, and language acquisition will be less problematic.

In fact, endorsing and acting on twin individuality is the greatest gift you can give to your children. To counter the attention twins receive as a pair, I suggest the following:

1. As early as possible, designate objects such as toys, games, friends, and clothes for each twin that cannot be shared without asking.
2. Discuss what is shared, and maintain sharing time.
3. Discipline each child separately to avoid twin enmeshment.

Barbara

Barbara Klein, Ph.D.
Twins and Gifted Children
Parent Coaching